HELLO
HELLO

To my assistant who helped me write *The Appleding.* —D. P.

For Anissa,

with whom I would go to sea in a Sieve

and happily live in a crockery-jar. —C. B.

Illustrations © 2011 by Calef Brown.
Introduction © 2011 by Daniel Pinkwater.
All rights reserved. No part of this book may be reproduced
in any form without written permission from the publisher.

Library of Congress Cataloging-in-Publication Data
Lear, Edward, 1812–1888.
His shoes were far too tight : poems / by Edward Lear ;
masterminded by Daniel Pinkwater and illustrated by Calef Brown.
p. cm.
ISBN 978-0-8118-6792-4
1. Children's poetry, English. 2. Nonsense verses, English.
I. Pinkwater, Daniel Manus, 1941–II. Brown, Calef. III. Title.
PR4879.L2H57 2011
821'.8—dc22
2010008549

Book design by Kristine Brogno.
Typeset in Gotham and Rockwell.
The illustrations in this book were rendered in acrylics.

Manufactured through Asia Pacific Offset by Power Printing,
Heyuan, China, in January 2011.

10 9 8 7 6 5 4 3 2 1

This product conforms to CPSIA 2008.

Chronicle Books LLC
680 Second Street, San Francisco, California 94107

www.chroniclekids.com

IMAGE CREDITS FOR INTRODUCTION:
Photo of Edward Lear: Carte-de-visite, 1862,
Mrs. R. E. C. Stileman

Drawings: from *Edward Lear: the Complete
Verse and Nonsense*, Penguin Books, 2001

HIS SHOES WERE FAR TOO TIGHT
BY EDWARD LEAR

Masterminded by Daniel Pinkwater

Illustrated by Calef Brown

chronicle books · san francisco

INTRODUCTION

He was a fat, goofy-looking guy with thick eyeglasses. He liked people, but he was shy. He liked kids. He liked animals. He had a cat named Old Foss. This is a picture he drew of himself:

HIS NAME WAS
EDWARD LEAR.

He was born a long time ago—almost 200 years. Mr. Lear was a good artist. He did a famous book of illustrations of parrots, painted landscapes, and even gave drawing lessons to Queen Victoria. (This didn't last long, possibly because his behavior was too silly to allow him to hang around the royal court.)

Because he was shy and had health problems all his life, Mr. Lear kept to himself, which meant he got to observe people from a distance. He may have noticed that

ADULTS ARE A BIT RIDICULOUS.

He could see the funny side of things—and not just funny, he saw how nice it is when things don't make sense in the way we are taught to expect them to make sense. He called this nonsense.

When Edward Lear was small, books for kids usually told how if you were not a "good child"—quiet, obedient, and hard-working—you would starve to death or be eaten by wild wolves. But in his lifetime, books for children changed, and people began to make books that were supposed to be entertaining and even funny.

MR. LEAR LOVED TO MAKE NONSENSE POEMS.

The first ones were published in a book in 1846. Kids, and adults who are not too serious, have loved them ever since. We have picked a few, and added paintings by Calef Brown.

(I think Mr. Lear would have liked them.)

SO, TURN THE PAGE, AND MEET MR. LEAR.

HOW PLEASANT TO KNOW MR. LEAR!

How pleasant to know Mr. Lear!
Who has written such volumes of stuff!
Some think him ill-tempered and queer,
But a few think him pleasant enough.

His mind is concrete and fastidious;
His nose is remarkably big;
His visage is more or less hideous;
His beard it resembles a wig.

He has ears, and two eyes, and ten fingers,
Leastways if you reckon two thumbs;
Long ago he was one of the singers,
But now he is one of the dumbs.

He sits in a beautiful parlor,
With hundreds of books on the wall;
He drinks a great deal of Marsala,
But never gets tipsy at all.

He has many friends, lay men and clerical;
Old Foss is the name of his cat;
His body is perfectly spherical;
He weareth a runcible hat.

When he walks in waterproof white
The children run after him so!
Calling out, "He's come out in his night-
Gown, that crazy old Englishman, O!"

He weeps by the side of the ocean,
He weeps on the top of the hill;
He purchases pancakes and lotion,
And chocolate shrimps from the mill.

He reads, but he cannot speak, Spanish;
He cannot abide ginger beer.
Ere the days of his pilgrimage vanish,
How pleasant to know Mr. Lear!

THE POBBLE WHO HAS NO TOES

I

The Pobble who has no toes
Had once as many as we;
When they said, "Some day you may lose them all;"
He replied, "Fish fiddle de-dee!"
And his Aunt Jobiska made him drink
Lavender water tinged with pink,
For she said, "The World in general knows
There's nothing so good for a Pobble's toes!"

II

The Pobble who has no toes,
Swam across the Bristol Channel;
But before he set out he wrapped his nose
In a piece of scarlet flannel.
For his Aunt Jobiska said, "No harm
Can come to his toes if his nose is warm;
And it's perfectly known that a Pobble's toes
Are safe—provided he minds his nose."

III

The Pobble swam fast and well
And when boats or ships came near him
He tinkedly-binkledy-winkled a bell
So that all the world could hear him.
And all the Sailors and Admirals cried,
When they saw him nearing the further side,
"He has gone to fish for his Aunt Jobiska's
Runcible Cat with crimson whiskers!"

IV

But before he touched the shore,
The shore of the Bristol Channel,
A sea-green Porpoise carried away
His wrapper of scarlet flannel.
And when he came to observe his feet,
Formerly garnished with toes so neat,
His face at once became forlorn
On perceiving that all his toes were gone!

THE OWL AND THE PUSSYCAT

I

The Owl and the Pussy-cat went to sea
In a beautiful pea green boat,
They took some honey, and plenty of money,
Wrapped up in a five pound note.
The Owl looked up to the stars above,
And sang to a small guitar,
"O lovely Pussy! O Pussy my love,
What a beautiful Pussy you are,
You are,
You are!
What a beautiful Pussy you are!"

II

Pussy said to the Owl, "You elegant fowl!
How charmingly sweet you sing!
O let us be married! too long we have tarried:
But what shall we do for a ring?"
They sailed away, for a year and a day,
To the land where the Bong-tree grows,
And there in a wood a Piggy-wig stood
With a ring at the end of his nose,
His nose,
His nose,
With a ring at the end of his nose.

III

"Dear pig, are you willing to sell for one shilling
Your ring?" Said the Piggy, "I will."
So they took it away, and were married next day
By the Turkey who lives on the hill.
They dined on mince, and slices of quince,
Which they ate with a runcible spoon;
And hand in hand, on the edge of the sand,
They danced by the light of the moon,
The moon,
The moon,
They danced by the light of the moon.

THE DUCK AND THE KANGAROO

Said the Duck to the Kangaroo,
"Good gracious! how you hop!
Over the fields and the water too,
As if you never would stop!
My life is a bore in this nasty pond,
And I long to go out in the world beyond!
I wish I could hop like you!"
Said the Duck to the Kangaroo.
"Please give me a ride on your back!"
Said the Duck to the Kangaroo.
"I would sit quite still, and say nothing but 'Quack,'
The whole of the long day through!
And we'd go to the Dee, and the Jelly Bo Lee,
Over the land and over the sea—
Please take me a ride! O do!"
Said the Duck to the Kangaroo.
Said the Kangaroo to the Duck,
"This requires some little reflection;
Perhaps on the whole it might bring me luck,
And there seems but one objection,
Which is, if you'll let me speak so bold,
Your feet are unpleasantly wet and cold,
And would probably give me the roo-
matiz!" said the Kangaroo.

Said the Duck, "As I sate on the rocks,
I have thought over that completely,
And I bought four pairs of worsted socks
Which fit my web-feet neatly.
And to keep out the cold I've bought a cloak,
And every day a cigar I'll smoke,
All to follow my own dear true
Love of a Kangaroo!"
Said the Kangaroo, "I'm ready!
All in the moonlight pale;
But to balance me well, dear Duck, sit steady!
And quite at the end of my tail!"
So away they went with a hop and a bound,
And they hopped the whole world three times round;
And who so happy—O who,
As the Duck and the Kangaroo?

THE JUMBLIES

I

They went to sea in a Sieve, they did,
In a Sieve they went to sea:
In spite of all their friends could say,
On a winter's morn, on a stormy day,
In a Sieve they went to sea!
And when the Sieve turned round and round,
And every one cried, "You'll all be drowned!"
They called aloud, "Our Sieve ain't big,
But we don't care a button! we don't care a fig!
In a Sieve we'll go to sea!"
Far and few, far and few,
Are the lands where the Jumblies live;
Their heads are green, and their hands are blue,
And they went to sea in a Sieve.

II

They sailed away in a Sieve, they did,
In a Sieve they sailed so fast,
With only a beautiful pea-green veil
Tied with a riband by way of a sail,
To a small tobacco-pipe mast;
And every one said, who saw them go,
"O won't they be soon upset, you know!
For the sky is dark, and the voyage is long,
And happen what may, it's extremely wrong
In a Sieve to sail so fast!"
Far and few, far and few,
Are the lands where the Jumblies live;
Their heads are green, and their hands are blue,
And they went to sea in a Sieve.

III

The water it soon came in, it did,
The water it soon came in;
So to keep them dry, they wrapped their feet
In a pinky paper all folded neat,
And they fastened it down with a pin.
And they passed the night in a crockery-jar,
And each of them said, "How wise we are!
Though the sky be dark, and the voyage be long,
Yet we never can think we were rash or wrong,
While round in our Sieve we spin!"
Far and few, far and few,
Are the lands where the Jumblies live;
Their heads are green, and their hands are blue,
And they went to sea in a Sieve.

IV

And all night long they sailed away
And when the sun went down,
They whistled and warbled a moony song
To the echoing sound of a coppery gong,
In the shade of the mountains brown.
"O Timballo! How happy we are,
When we live in a Sieve and a crockery-jar,
And all night long in the moonlight pale,
We sail away with a pea-green sail,
In the shade of the mountains brown!"
Far and few, far and few,
Are the lands where the Jumblies live;
Their heads are green, and their hands are blue,
And they went to sea in a Sieve.

V

They sailed to the Western Sea, they did,
To a land all covered with trees,
And they bought an Owl, and a useful Cart,
And a pound of Rice, and a Cranberry Tart,
And a hive of silvery Bees.
And they bought a Pig, and some green Jack-daws,
And a lovely Monkey with lollipop paws,
And forty bottles of Ring-Bo-Ree,
And no end of Stilton Cheese.
Far and few, far and few,
Are the lands where the Jumblies live;
Their heads are green, and their hands are blue,
And they went to sea in a Sieve.

VI

And in twenty years they all came back,
In twenty years or more,
And every one said, "How tall they've grown!
For they've been to the Lakes, and the Torrible Zone,
And the hills of the Chankly Bore!"
And they drank their health, and gave them a feast
Of dumplings made of beautiful yeast;
And every one said, "If we only live,
We too will go to sea in a Sieve—
To the hills of the Chankly Bore!"
Far and few, far and few,
Are the lands where the Jumblies live;
Their heads are green, and their hands are blue,
And they went to sea in a Sieve.

THE QUANGLE WANGLE'S HAT

I

On the top of the Crumpetty Tree
The Quangle Wangle sat,
But his face you could not see,
On account of his Beaver Hat.
For his hat was a hundred and two feet wide,
With ribbons and bibbons on every side
And bells, and buttons, and loops, and lace,
So that nobody ever could see the face
Of the Quangle Wangle Quee.

II

The Quangle Wangle said
To himself on the Crumpetty Tree,—
"Jam; and jelly; and bread;
Are the best food for me!
But the longer I live on this Crumpetty Tree
The plainer that ever it seems to me
That very few people come this way
And that life on the whole is far from gay!"
Said the Quangle Wangle Quee.

III

But there came to the Crumpetty Tree,
Mr. and Mrs. Canary;
And they said, "Did you ever see
Any spot so charmingly airy?
May we build a nest on your lovely Hat?
Mr. Quangle Wangle, grant us that!
O please let us come and build a nest
Of whatever material suits you best,
Mr. Quangle Wangle Quee!"

IV

And besides, to the Crumpetty Tree
Came the Stork, the Duck, and the Owl;
The Snail, and the Bumble-Bee,
The Frog, and the Fimble Fowl;
(The Fimble Fowl, with a Corkscrew leg;)
And all of them said, "We humbly beg,
We may build our homes on your lovely Hat,
Mr. Quangle Wangle, grant us that!
Mr. Quangle Wangle Quee!"

V

And the Golden Grouse came there,
And the Pobble who has no toes,
And the small Olympian bear,
And the Dong with a luminous nose.
And the Blue Baboon, who played the flute,
And the Orient Calf from the Land of Tute,
And the Attery Squash, and the Bisky Bat,
All came and built on the lovely Hat
Of the Quangle Wangle Quee.

VI

And the Quangle Wangle said
To himself on the Crumpetty Tree,—
"When all these creatures move
What a wonderful noise there'll be!"
And at night by the light of the Mulberry moon
They danced to the flute of the Blue Baboon,
On the broad green leaves of the Crumpetty Tree,
And all were as happy as happy could be,
With the Quangle Wangle Quee.

MRS. BLUE DICKEY BIRD

Mrs. Blue Dickey-bird, who went out a-walking with her six chickey birds;
    she carried a parasol and wore a bonnet of green silk.
The first little chickey bird had daisies growing out of his head and wore boots
    because of the dirt.
The second little chickey bird wore a hat for fear it should rain.
The third little chickey bird carried a jug of water.
The fourth little chickey bird carried a muff, to keep her wings warm.
The fifth little chickey bird was round as a ball.
And the sixth little chickey bird walked on his head to save his feet.

SOME INCIDENTS IN THE LIFE OF MY UNCLE ARLY

I

O! My agèd Uncle Arly!
Sitting on a heap of Barley
Thro' the silent hours of night,
Close beside a leafy thicket:
On his nose there was a Cricket,
In his hat a Railway Ticket;
(But his shoes were far too tight.)

II

Long ago, in youth, he squander'd
All his goods away, and wander'd
To the Tiniskoop-hills afar.
There on golden sunsets blazing,
Every morning found him gazing,
Singing, "Orb! you're quite amazing!
How I wonder what you are!"

III

Like the ancient Medes and Persians,
Always by his own exertions
He subsisted on those hills;
Whiles, by teaching children spelling,
Or at times by merely yelling,
Or at intervals by selling
'Propter's Nicodemus Pills.'

IV

Later, in his morning rambles
He perceived the moving brambles
Something square and white disclose;
'Twas a First-class Railway Ticket;
But, on stooping down to pick it
Off the ground, a pea-green Cricket
settled on my uncle's Nose.

V

Never—never more, Oh! never,
Did that Cricket leave him ever,
Dawn or evening, day or night;
Clinging as a constant treasure,
Chirping with a cheerious measure,
Wholly to my uncle's pleasure
(Though his shoes were far too tight.)

VI

So for three-and-forty winters,
Till his shoes were worn to splinters,
All those hills he wander'd o'er,
Sometimes silent, sometimes yelling;
Till he came to Borley-Melling,
Near his old ancestral dwelling;
(But his shoes were far too tight.)

VII

On a little heap of Barley
Died my agèd uncle Arly,
And they buried him one night;
Close beside the leafy thicket;
There, his hat and Railway Ticket;
There, his ever-faithful Cricket;
(But his shoes were far too tight.)

NONSENSE ALPHABET

A was an ape,
Who stole some white tape,
And tied up his toes
In four beautiful bows.
A!
Funny old ape!

B was a bat,
Who slept all the day,
And fluttered about
When the sun went away.
B!
Brown little bat!

C was a camel:
You rode on his hump;
And if you fell off,
You came down such a bump!
C!
What a high camel!

D was a dove,
Who lived in a wood,
With such pretty soft wings,
And so gentle and good!
D!
Dear little dove!

E was an eagle,
Who sat on the rocks,
And looked down on the fields
And the-far-away flocks.
E!
Beautiful eagle!

F was a fan
Made of beautiful stuff;
And when it was used,
It went puffy-puff-puff!
F!
Nice little fan!

G was a gooseberry,
Perfectly red;
To be made into jam,
And eaten with bread.
G!
Gooseberry red!

H

H was a heron,
Who stood in a stream:
The length of his neck
And his legs was extreme.

H!

Long-legged heron!

I

I was an inkstand,
Which stood on a table,
With a nice pen to write with
When we are able.

I!

Neat little inkstand!

J

J was a jug,
So pretty and white,
With fresh water in it
At morning and night.

J!

Nice little jug!

K was a kingfisher:
Quickly he flew,
So bright and so pretty!—
Green, purple, and blue.
K!
Kingfisher blue!

L was a lily,
So white and so sweet!
To see it and smell it
Was quite a nice treat.
L!
Beautiful lily!

M was a man,
Who walked round and round;
And he wore a long coat
That came down to the ground.
M!
Funny old man!

N was a nut
So smooth and so brown!
And when it was ripe,
It fell tumble-dum-down.
N!
Nice little nut!

O was an oyster,
Who lived in his shell:
If you let him alone,
He felt perfectly well.
O!
Open-mouthed oyster!

P was a polly,
All red, blue, and green—
The most beautiful polly
That ever was seen.
P!
Poor little polly!

Q was a quill
Made into a pen;
But I do not know where,
And I cannot say when.
Q!
Nice little quill!

R was a rattlesnake,
Rolled up so tight,
Those who saw him ran quickly,
For fear he should bite.
R!
Rattlesnake bite!

S was a screw
To screw down a box;
And then it was fastened
Without any locks.
S!
Valuable screw!

T was a thimble,
Of silver so bright!
When placed on the finger,
It fitted so tight!
T!
Nice little thimble!

U was an upper-coat,
Woolly and warm,
To wear over all
In the snow or the storm.
U!
What a nice upper-coat!

V was a veil
With a border upon it,
And a ribbon to tie it
All round a pink bonnet.
V!
Pretty green veil!

W was a watch,
Where, in letters of gold,
The hour of the day
You might always behold.
W!
Beautiful watch!

X was King Xerxes,
Who wore on his head
A mighty large turban,
Green, yellow, and red.
X!
Look at King Xerxes!

Y was a yak,
From the land of Thibet:
Except his white tail,
He was all black as jet.
Y!
Look at the yak!

Z was a zebra,
All striped white and black;
And if he were tame,
You might ride on his back.
z!
Pretty striped zebra!

THERE WAS AN OLD DERRY DOWN DERRY

There was an old Derry down Derry, who loved to see little folks merry;
So he made them a book, and with laughter they shook
At the fun of that Derry down Derry.